Beyond Valentine's Day

BOOK #3

mind diet

Steve Jaffe

THE
MIND
DIET®
GROUP, INC.

Beyond Valentine's Day, Making Love All Year Long

ISBN: 0-9720605-2-9

Published by

THE
MDG MIND DIET®
GROUP, INC.

2217 Levante Street
Carlsbad, CA 92009

Tel: 760.436.7253
Fax: 760.436.6608

E-mail: Aminddiet@aol.com
Web: www.aminddiet.com
www.aminddiet.com

DEDICATION

Being in love or trying to build a loving relationship comes with no rulebooks to guide you through the maze of confusion that awaits you. It takes effort, care and trust continuously with an open heart to give 100% of who you are to make your relationship work.

I dedicate this book of love to everyone who has dreamed of living within a storybook relationship and has been detoured along the way. It can be done if you really want it to happen. It happened to me on November 10, 1990.

TABLE OF CONTENTS

54

Chapter Three

LOVING YOUR TIME TOGETHER

74

Chapter Four

NEVER LET THE PASSION STOP

90

WHAT TO DO NEXT

OTHER BOOKS IN THE MIND DIET SERIES

1. *Count Your Life With Smiles, Not Tears*
    ISBN: 0-9720605-0-2
    $16.95

    Count Your Life With Smiles, Not Tears is an inter-
    active guide to tackling life's challenges–from daily
    pressures to financial worries to romantic relation-
    ships–through the use of rhythm poetry.

    Steve Jaffe combines compassion and understanding
    with his easy-to-follow format of poetry exercises.
    He offers himself as an example and speaks from
    experience, revealing the liberating power of rhythm
    poetry. Going a step further than traditional journaling, Jaffe turns each
    experience into an opportunity to learn–and move your life along.

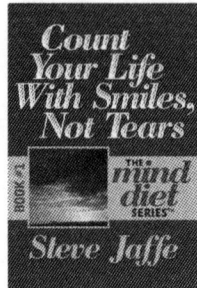

2. *Healing From Within, Emotionally Surviving Cancer*
    ISBN: 0-9720605-1-0
    $14.95

    Doctors can treat the cancer, but keeping emotional
    health strong all-too-frequently falls on the shoul-
    ders of the patient enduring cancer treatment. In
    Healing From Within: Emotionally Surviving
    Cancer Steve Jaffe offers a helping hand to anyone
    fighting cancer by teaching how to write through the
    fear and the pain that inevitably accompany it.

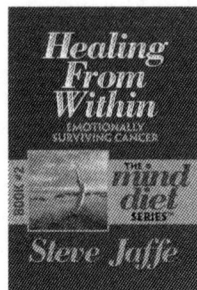

The Mind Diet Series **books are available everwhere books are sold.
To purchase books online, visit: www.aminddiet.com.**

FUTURE MIND DIET
SERIES BOOKS

A NOTE TO ALL LOVERS
AND FUTURE LOVERS

To be able to touch someone's heart, to massage it with your words can be the most rewarding experience two people can have. A giver and a receiver if the love is truly there will play a ping-pong sort of loving game giving each other everyday the gift of making love.

Being in love for a day, a week, a year, or fifty years, doesn't prevent you from taking a risk to express loving emotions everyday. "Practice makes perfect", and that is what this book is designed to do. I want to guide you toward freely letting your emotions escape into beautiful sounding words.

You might be in a relationship that feels one sided where only one of the partners expresses without effort their loving emotions. The relationship is possibly great in most respects, but missing the back and forth communication that is needed to keep that special spark igniting the passion that brought you together. This observation is not a notice to panic, or that you are not feeling a unique love for the person you are spending time with. The expression of feelings are controlled by how our past has affected us.

This book will not be a lesson on how to build a loving relationship, but a playful tool to excite your relationship with communication—both verbal and physical.

It's possible, at this precise moment in your life, that you've had some really bad experiences when you tried to express your feelings, and had your heart hurt. Maybe you don't have anything to draw upon from your childhood. Your parents might not have expressed their feelings for each other in front of you. It didn't mean they weren't in love, they just kept it private. And although you may express your feelings, your partner may not reciprocate in the way you want him/her to.

The book *Beyond Valentine's Day, The Perpetual Lover* is a compilation of love poems that I had created for my best friend and wife, Nancy. I want to share them with you, with the goal of guiding each of you so you can learn a wonderful way to express your love and build a stronger, more lasting relationship.

I believe that two people in love can make love all day long. Not with sex, but with emotions. Believe me, that when you speak from your heart, everything you do in your relationship grows to new, wonderful levels. Sex becomes another warm loving expression of your feelings, allowing you to look deep into your lovers eyes so you can experience that warm magnificent moment together.

The chapters will act as your guideline to achieving what I believe are Mind Diet Experiences that make your day-to-day existence glorious. You will have the opportunity to learn what a Mind Diet is and how to practice it with your partner. This book will be different from my other books as you and your partner will share the book, picking the poems you like and writing your own feelings adjacent to the poem you chose. At the end of the book I have included a "Promise Contract," which both partners need to complete and sign. I want this book to be an emotional photo album of your love so you can, when times get difficult, go back to and remember the passion that you both once felt. I have written other books that deal with loss, pain, and life threatening diseases. However, this book will focus only on love and keeping the flame burning bright and long.

INTRODUCTION TO
A MIND DIET PHILOSOPHY

To explain what A MIND DIET is, would be like trying to explain a beautiful sunset, or a warm hug, or a non-stop belly laugh. It was meant to be that way because a Mind Diet is something that begins inside your brain and controls every part of your body. However, a definition might be a good starting point, as you search for your own meaning of what a Mind Diet is for you, in your relationship. The definition will expand as you become more involved in your search.

> MIND DIET®: *The precise moment when your mind and body quivers, gets goose bumps and at the same time your thoughts get lost in the moment and a rush of exhilarated emotions takes over.*

Each person experiences life's thrills from different perspectives. Understanding this one point can improve a relationship instantly.

Can you recall a time or an occasion, when a rush of adrenaline swept over your body that came from a wonderful time or special split second? Did it make you smile, laugh, cry for joy? Did it feel great to communicate your feelings with someone who understood you, the moment you realized someone really listened? Or did you just witness a sunrise or sunset and felt a warm stillness flow through your body? Those are all MIND DIETS!

Should you strive to experience A MIND DIET every moment of your life? I personally think so. Experiencing a Mind Diet alone is perfectly wonderful, but when you have the opportunity to share that moment with someone close, your feelings are unmatched by anything you have ever felt. We all have a need to share, so why not experience a Mind Diet with that special someone?

Not every day will be a Mind Diet type of day. Life just won't allow it to happen. Our day-to-day problems, moods, or just our body chemistry just won't allow our minds to release us from those troublesome moments. In my opinion, you should not avoid those difficult times in your life. Burying your head in the sand only avoids dealing with life. Problems, pains, fears and loss, do not go away by escaping. Some people turn to alcohol, smoking, and even drugs, as their Mind Diet. Those tools do not relieve their problems; they only compound the difficulties that are plaguing you.

YOUR LIFE IS LIKE A WHEEL

Picture your life as a wheel with as many spokes as you need to keep your wheel perfectly round. Visualize each spoke as an illustration of everything good and bad in your life. Once you see the current factors that sum up your life, then you can find the weak spokes to repair. Soon your wheel will roll smoothly on your journey. This is the philosophy I preach in all of my books.

Beyond Valentine's Day, The Perpetual Lover, assumes that you are in love with your partner. The only work you'll be doing is exploring the warm caring feelings inside your heart, touching upon areas that never existed

Please understand that practicing the MIND DIET Program, could help strengthen some of your weak spokes to make your relationship roll smoothly.

When you have those unpleasant periods in your life, search for those *Mind Diet Experiences,* and try to share them with your partner. Try to tell your lover at least ten times a day how much you love her/him. It's a great habit to get into. Use words that paint a wonderful image of how you are feeling.

The heart of this book is to use poems to strengthen who you are and how to improve your romantic life each day. We have only this life to make the most out of, and right now can be the best time to begin to turn up that loving flame you have inside yourself.

The poems you will read have been designed to motivate and stimulate your mind and thoughts. They are only examples. They will help you communicate first, with yourself, then with your spouse, a best friend, or someone very close to you. You will eventually develop a magical rhythm to where you will be able to write your own poems to release your feelings. If instead of writing a poem, you write your feelings, then you've accomplished what this book wanted for you. Don't worry about having an instant rhythm at first—it will come as your mind begins to lose its excess weight. My first poems were very different than my present poems.

SUGGESTIONS ON TRYING THIS PROGRAM

Express your love unconditionally,
never expecting anything in return.
Your words are like a magic potion
and will ignite a flame within your lover.
A relationship can only work
if you want it to work.

The *MIND DIET PROGRAM* is not a cure-all for a bad relationship. It is a tool for you to use so you can learn to express those important feelings, which tell your partner how much you truly love them. I love giving my wife gifts for no special reason (except to say I love you), and in lieu of a greeting card I attach a poem or words that express my love.

At first, you will just write your feelings. Then as you become comfortable you will automatically find your rhythm and watch a poem bloom that expresses your true loving feelings.

One last and crucial point that I need to mention before you start on your Mind Diet journey is: *This book is just for you and your partner.* Don't become judgmental or critical of how your significant other expresses their feelings. Appreciate that they have expressed them and embrace the words with all of your love. While we have always searched for some fairy tale type of loving relationship, it was created by outside stimuli. Use this book to create your own true fairy tale love story.

I wish you the best during your life, and remember:
Your relationship is like a song, so sing it all day long.

PRACTICING THE MIND
DIET PROGRAM

At first, the attempt at writing your feelings down will come about privately. While I suggest you read the poems together, you might at first feel more at ease going somewhere private to write the thoughts that you want to share. It is perfectly acceptable to write your feeling, your poems and not share them right away. If communication before you started this book was difficult, patience and understanding will have to be granted at the beginning. One partner might have more openness and will share their feelings first. Both partners should reassure themselves that it is perfectly all right.

As a boy growing-up, I came from an environment that frowned upon expressing ones feelings openly. Anger, putdowns, and foul language were the only forms of expression I grew up with. "Men were to be strong and show no weaknesses," was preached by most of the male role models in my family. I thank my grandfather and mother for teaching me that a man can be strong *and* manly *and* still express emotions in a loving and caring manner. I thank Nancy, my wonderful wife, who never disapproves of how I choose to express my love toward her.

To all men who are reading this book, be willing to try something outside of your comfort zone and attempt to express your love toward your partner differently than you've done in the past. Women, have patience with your partner, they have a lot of baggage that needs unpacking and repacking to move past the difficult hurdles they have.

I suggest that you find a relaxing time in your day to practice. If both of you work, it can be done by getting up thirty minutes earlier, or during a lunch break, or before dinner. The important thing is to make the time to involve yourself in *Making Love All Year Long*. Become your own creation of a perpetual lover.

*Be inventive with your words and go beyond
the old limits you had set for yourself.*

No one can teach you how to express yourself, except you. There might be times when you can't find the words, but can find the setting to show your love. A walk in a park, a stroll barefoot in the sand, a picnic, waking your partner up early to witness a gorgeous sunrise are other thoughtful ways to make love. Don't measure your relationship by the frequency of sexual interplay, but by the frequency of the emotional lovemaking you do. Sex is the dessert after a gourmet meal; so don't rush it.

Don't feel inadequate if your partner picks up the rhythm part of writing faster than you. It doesn't mean they are more emotional or more in tuned with what is going on. The ability to write your feelings down on a piece of paper is the accomplishment.

Remember why you fell in love in the first place and use The Mind Diet Program to stoke your emotional fire. Be committed to seeing your life from new eyes and fall in love everyday and plan a life together one filled with Mind Diets. It is not expensive to be romantic, only creative.

The next two poems are examples of what I wrote five years ago and the feelings I wrote about it. Use this as a guideline to begin to express how you feel. I had created an anniversary poem book that was mixed not only with poems, but other emotional feelings that could not be expressed with poetry.

Chapter One
THE AWAKENING

FOOD FOR THOUGHT FOR YOUR NEW BEGINNINGS

Start this chapter by making a list of various places where you'd like to be romantic. Make a list of the beautiful attributes your partner has, and, then make a list of the emotions you are feeling at this moment toward your partner. This will stimulate your mind and heart to begin to express those hidden feelings.

ROMANTIC PLACES:

1. _____

2. _____

3. _____

4. _____

5. _____

6. _____

7. _____

8. _____

9. _____

10. _____

BEAUTIFUL ATTRIBUTES OF
MY PARTNER:

1. _____
2. _____
3. _____
4. _____
5. _____
6. _____
7. _____
8. _____
9. _____
10. _____

MY EMOTIONS PRESENTLY TOWARD
MY RELATIONSHIP:

1. _____
2. _____
3. _____
4. _____
5. _____
6. _____
7. _____
8. _____
9. _____
10. _____

Use your lists to help you plan your lovemaking. Your day-to-day demands will try to get in your way and pressure you to put this book on the shelf. Don't let it. Practice for a minimum of 21 days in a row, so it can become a normal habit.

Try to call your partner at least five times throughout your day, to tell him or her how much you love them. Try to leave them a loving note in a place you know they will look at sometime during their day. This could be in a briefcase, a coat pocket, on a car seat, under a pillow, on a dinner plate, pasted to a door that they will use when they come home. This is a way of making love that builds toward a stronger trusting relationship.

"WHAT I FEEL"

I take a breath and fill my lungs
with the love I feel for you,
I am no longer alone without purpose,
these feelings are very true.

You are my teacher of how to be,
the man I was destined to fulfill,
allowing me to experience a world,
that's filled with you through and through.

Your patience and care
ease me through
the world of challenges I face,
I owe you oh so much,
without you I might break.

Our time so far has been so brief,
but filled with a life time of joy,
I am looking forward everyday
for the continued experiences
with you that I will enjoy.

Each point in time builds for me
a foundation of love for you,
and every anniversary is our mark
of what we've been struggling through.

MY EMOTINAL FEELINGS

WHAT YOU MEAN TO ME:

Our beginnings were made from all our past experiences and the mix of our good, became our relationship. The excitement of our newness gave us a high that was not ever experienced by us before.

A certain trust was formed that removed all expectations for our relationship so no roadblocks would be felt as we fell in love.

Each day with you is like a song, rhyming and pleasant to my ears. It repeats and repeats until a new song is felt and my mind just sings our love all day long.

Our time together has been so short, but a life time of experiences have been completed. It has formed a bond that I have for you and what my life is becoming.

As you read each of these poems, please feel the love I have for you. I have never expressed my inner feeling to anyone as I am doing in this book. This is my lasting gift to you for all that you do for me.

Your Loving Husband and Friend

- *Steve*

"WHERE ARE WE GOING?"

It's unknown this trip we're on,
it moves in mysterious ways,
changing it's direction,
each and every day.
What is so great, is that we both,
participate in its plan,
always finding ways to enjoy,
as we hold each others hand.

Our trip will never end,
as it circles our daily lives,
and forcing us to always come back,
to where we once arrived.

As our years drift on,
and we change our plans,
it should never cause concern,
as a change is only a new beginning for us,
to experience, love, and learn.

So come with me and journey beyond
the experiences you once thought great,
and be assured that what I've planned
will seem like our first date.

Where we are going,
I do not know
or when it will ever end,
but come with me and see our world
as my only true best friend.

MY EMOTIONAL FEELINGS

OUR FUTURE IS UNKNOWN:

It is so exciting wondering what our next day, week, month or year will be like. From our first day together, there has never been a moment that I would not want to repeat.

Everything I do with you is fun, exciting and an adventure. The world has truly become my playground and you my playmate.

Where all of this will go, I do not know or care to know. I have so much trust that whatever we do will be the most loving and wonderful time of my life.

I look forward to all our adventures.

"WORKING AS A TEAM"

A team knows every move,
its players need to make,
to make the team successful to achieve,
without creating costly mistakes.
We are a team that knows what goes,
on inside our heads,
and anticipates the correct thing to do,
before a word is said.

To anticipate each others thoughts,
comes from a deep love we have inside,
that tells the other person we love,
about the level of our pride.
It's not the expectations,
nor desires we care to instill,
but a melding of our souls,
so we can be fulfilled.

Our team has no captain
or leader to guide us through,
we just give our hearts permission,
to make our dreams come true.
So always let your heart escape
to that joyous state of being,
and it will make our goals achieve,
exactly what we are dreaming.

We are a team that appears as one,
but has the strength of two,
it cannot ever be defeated,
no matter what we do.

Personal Emotions

_____

_____

_____

_____

_____

_____

_____

_____

_____

_____

_____

_____

_____

_____

_____

_____

_____

_____

_____

_____

_____

_____

"ALL MY DREAMS"

Today I dream of what will be,
and what I want in my life,
and it always come around to you,
the dream of you as my wife.
I can not think without it including,
your hand gripped tight with mine,
as I travel through my dreams,
that take me oh so far beyond.

A dream can be a wish at times,
but mine seem quite so real,
the feelings in my heart sing out
no longer dreams are what I feel.

At times I day dream of places to be,
or things to accomplish real soon,
but always in my wonderful dreams,
is the picture of only you.

My dreams are really my plans for us,
so you can feel quite pleased,
that you have someone in your life,
that will let you be released.

So release yourself and be the woman,
you wish to have for you,
so I can experience the true woman you are
as I journey together with you.

Personal Emotions

"WHEN FRIENDSHIP BECOMES A RELATIONSHIP"

There is a magic that goes on,
when you have that special friend,
and being with them is the best time,
you have over and over again.
It's ok to make your friendship,
become a loving one,
you'll know it's supposed to happen,
as your time keeps moving on.

When being close connects your hearts,
and makes you embrace your feelings,
it's time to peel off your masks,
and begin to start revealing.
A friendship has a certain bond,
that will see you through this time,
and allow you the moment to experience a love,
that was so hard to find.

So let your heart dictate for you,
the love you want to feel,
and make that special friendship you have,
become a relationship that's real.
A life time commitment should be your goal
to treasure your special friend,
and let your heart build that special relationship
that will never have to end.

Personal Emotions

"PARTNERS FOR LIFE"

When we said, "I love you",
that's when our contract began,
a partnership for life,
working hand in hand as friends.

We seek the goals that will blend with our hearts,
and work together as one.
Shielding each other from obstacles that aim,
to hinder and to harm.

We know each other's thoughts at times
and react to make it so,
and bring on a smile,
that makes our faces glow.

It's love we have for this partnership,
its unwritten contract guides us through,
but what makes this a wonderful deal,
is sharing it all with you.

Personal Emotions

_____
_____
_____
_____
_____
_____
_____
_____
_____
_____
_____
_____
_____
_____
_____
_____
_____
_____
_____
_____
_____
_____

"A RELATIONSHIP BUILT ON STRENGTH"

Each moment we take to be close to our hearts,
creates a foundation that forms all around,
we are protected by this force
that makes our love so strong.

From the day we began, to the day I said "I do",
I have never doubted the love we have,
each moment that I spend in your warm glowing rays,
make me thankful I am your friend.

On the day we tied our knot, I gave a special gift,
that was to build a foundation of my love,
that I promised would never quit.

Today that promise is just as strong
as it was the first day we met
and I will always continue to love you
and try to do my best.

Personal Emotions

"I WOULDN'T HAVE MISSED THIS FOR THE WORLD!"

The day you called to connect with me,
brought down the curtain of my past.
It was the beginning of pleasures to come,
a future that was meant to last.

I could have found a thousand things
to prevent our relationship to grow,
but you just cast your spell on me
and taught me a love I did not know.

I wouldn't have missed this for the world,
your beauty is a gift from God,
you continue to bless me with the experiences,
that makes my heart just throb.

I want to continue to celebrate,
this love I have inside,
and share with you the dreams I see,
in our future that's so alive.
So always smile and see me true,
I love you so unconditionally,
I will always be in love with you,
through of all eternity.

Personal Emotions

TRAINING EXERCISES

It is time to evaluate your own personal progress up to this point. Below are a few questions that you need to answer and then share them with your partner.

1. WHAT CHANGES HAVE YOU NOTICED IN YOURSELF?

2. HOW ARE YOU SEEING YOUR RELATIONSHIP?

3. WHAT WOULD YOU LIKE TO SEE HAPPEN OVER THE NEXT FEW WEEKS?

4. HOW HAS YOUR PARTNER CHANGED?

1. WHAT CHANGES HAVE YOU NOTICED IN YOURSELF

_____

_____

_____

_____

_____

_____

_____

_____

_____

_____

_____

_____

_____

_____

_____

_____

_____

_____

_____

2. HOW ARE YOU SEEING YOUR RELATIONSHIP?

_____

_____

_____

_____

_____

_____

_____

_____

_____

_____

_____

_____

_____

_____

_____

_____

_____

_____

_____

3. WHAT WOULD YOU LIKE TO SEE HAPPEN OVER THE NEXT FEW WEEKS?

_____

_____

_____

_____

_____

_____

_____

_____

_____

_____

_____

_____

_____

_____

_____

4. HOW HAS YOUR PARTNER CHANGED?

_____

_____

_____

_____

_____

_____

_____

_____

_____

_____

_____

_____

_____

_____

_____

_____

_____

_____

Chapter Two
GOOSEBUMPS

GOOSEBUMPS are one of the most sensual moments in a relationship. It is a special comfort zone that your partner puts you into. It can be a touch, a loving word or action, or just something spontaneous.

In a majority of relationships, Goosebumps go unnoticed. They become fleeting seconds that blow on by like a hurricane wind. They're gone in a flash.

The purpose of this chapter is to get both of you to slow down, and let the Goosebumps penetrate your heart and body, leaving a warm lasting impression. Our sensory abilities have been altered over the years by the media, work pressures, and family pressures.

Our Goosebumps chapter will attempt to alter your old sensory habits and create new ones. Not new ones entirely, but help you find the loving sensory feelings you once had.

Before you start this chapter make a list of all the things your partner can do for you that would get you Goosebumps. Some examples below will help jumpstart this exercise.

I remember when I first started dating my wife, Nancy; the smallest thoughtful things would make her happy to the point of crying. While I know it gave her Goosebumps, it gave me Goosebumps also. From there I kept enjoying the feelings I got when I saw her happy. To this day I continue to surprise her with unexpected loving thoughts. Men if you haven't thought of being perpetually romantic, you do not know what you are missing.

It takes two to keep the flame of love burning with passion and intensity. Being married for just one year or sixty years should not slow down the infatuation inside your heart toward your partner. Begin to make your list right now and witness the exciting transformation your relationship will take.

1.   A light, unexpected touch on the back of the neck or arm.
2.   A surprise phone call that tells you how much he or she loves you.
3.   (Men only on this one) Surprise your partner with a romantic dinner. Even if you can't cook, there are many supermarkets,

restaurants, or specialty stores that have dinners ready to just be warmed up. Do that with a nice candle and you've created great Goosebumps.

4. Plan a spontaneous picnic.
5. Set up a romantic dinner at one of your favorite restaurants.
6. Cuddle on the couch.
7. Watch a sunrise or sunset together.
8. Buy your partner a gift for no reason.
9. Give each other a loving relaxing massage.
10. Do one of your partner's normal chores without being asked.
11. Shampoo your partner's hair in the shower. Just do that and see how wonderful the experience will be.

Your list can be endless and that is the point. Invent your own Goosebump like items and practice them continually. Have fun with the next set of poems.

MY LIST OF GOOSEBUMPS

_____

_____

_____

_____

_____

_____

_____

_____

_____

"A HEART THAT'S OPEN"

To open a heart is not a natural thing,
it wants to protect itself,
but as I allowed myself to open up,
your soul found a place in my heart.

As trust builds within
and allows emotions to come out,
the entwining of our love seems to fill.
We both appear to be as happy
as two can ever be,
enjoying and being ourselves
it's just how it's supposed to be.

The opening of ones heart
is a secret few ever know,
but I am blessed we know this secret
as our love continues to grow.

I give you my heart to take in your hands
to do with as you please,
it's yours forever to love and care
that's how I want it to be.

Personal Emotions

"WORDS INTO ACTIONS"

As I say I love you,
are my actions true to form,
or do I just say the words
to string you quite along?

I have a responsibility,
to show you how I feel,
and bring you goosebumps that reflect,
a thrill of just what's real.

My actions come easily,
due to the amount of love I have,
and will always express and show to you
the feelings that will not make you so sad.

So check me out and listen close
and be open for my feel,
because the love I have for you
is oh so very real.

Personal Emotions

_____

_____

_____

_____

_____

_____

_____

_____

_____

_____

_____

_____

_____

_____

_____

_____

_____

_____

_____

_____

_____

_____

_____

"WHEN I THINK OF YOU"

*My thoughts of you come into my heart,
like the sunrise of our day,
and stays with me throughout my time,
and never drifts away.*

*These thoughts are such
that its reflection shows,
throughout my daily world,
and makes me appreciate the life I have,
with the most wonderful, caring girl.*

*It's hard to tell if a girl exists
or a woman that has experienced years,
you bring to me a playful mood,
that only I can share.*

*So when I think of only you
and call your lovely name,
or put you in my arms each day
the feelings are all the same,
it is the collection of my thoughts
that I treasure from now on,
and will only think of you each day,
these thoughts are never gone.*

Personal Emotions

"UNDERSTANDING THE CHANGES AROUND YOU"

What was once your norm, will change for you,
but don't let it affect your ways.
Just learn about the changes that are in a brew,
and grow with it along your way.

If "your love" goes through new changes,
see how you can help her not be blue,
these will become your changes also,
that will help you grow through and through.

There is a treasure to a change that appears,
if only you look real deep,
it is designed to bring out the beauty,
that builds your love for keeps.

If you feel a change is going on with you,
and is beginning to blend with "your loves,"
it's an opportunity to extend your emotions,
and build your internal love.

In a relationship there will always be
some change that will keep your currents running,
so don't try to rearrange or change your ways,
it's a start of a new beginning.
So enjoy this change of what you see
of the changes that's around,
so you can have a life of love
that will forever blossom and astound.

Personal Emotions

"TODAY AND TOMORROW"

Today is here to make you feel
a purpose for living your life today,
your dreams of tomorrow are your goals
you have to keep your relationship at play.

Without living today, there can be no tomorrows,
as your experiences are the roots for your goals,
so live all you can, so your dreams will be at hand
and you will have so many tomorrows to hold.

Today and Tomorrow go hand in hand
and cannot be attempted alone,
so work your todays with the dreams that you want,
and the tomorrows are there for you in your home.

Personal Emotions

"CAN I HAVE THIS DANCE?"

A dance is an act of emotion that you can do alone,
or with a group as one. Choosing to dance with someone you like
is not so difficult and can be done.

Sometimes it takes an ask of "may I,"
or the building of some trust,
but being able to dance with someone special, in life,
is a needed must.

There are too many people around who sit in a chair at a dance,
and always think that the next time,
is when they will take a chance.
But tomorrow never comes to us, unless today we try,
and that is what I did for me,
when I asked you to dance by my side.

Right away the dance had flow, we knew each others steps,
and found that all the types of dances, is what we did the best.
I am real glad I asked you to dance, and that you said it's ok,
there is no better way to love, than to dance with you all day.

As we dance a lot, our style will change
and the flow will become quite new,
so teach me all the new dance steps as I continue to love only you.
I promise to teach you in return the new steps that come to me,
and keeps us dancing all our lives
for all the world to see.

Personal Emotions

"WHY I LOVE YOU"

You have this way about you that draws me in, you have a calming affect on me. Your eyes look deep into my heart, that only I can see.

Your care, your touch affects me so, that my heart jumps up and down, I build a warm emotional feeling that never seems to come down.

You let me be a man to you and love my habits too, but most of all you show your love no matter what I do.

There are no conditions that I must do, or rules that have to be complete, you always show your love to me, I feel so totally complete.

So please don't ever reduce your love or stop expressing it so, it is an important part of you that makes me love you so.

There is a beauty that you possess, that make you act so free, I like that you expose yourself for only me to see.

The woman you are is what I love, it is a part of my soul, and when I see you fulfill yourself that's when I love you so

Personal Emotions

"WHY I STARE AT YOU"

A beautiful painting or sculpture needs a careful eye, to capture its total beauty, before your stare becomes a sigh.

I stare at you as much as I can and take in as much as I can see, but each time I stop to look at you, there is a new beauty that is revealed to me.

Your beauty is like the seasons, or a sunset blended with clouds, I just need to stare at what I see as my heart beats, oh so loud.

I never get tired of staring or thinking how lucky I am, I love the beauty of who you are, and will stare as your loving man.

Personal Emotions

"WHEN I LOOK AT YOU"

A warmth flows through my veins each time,
my eyes see your smiling face,
the glow you send into my life,
fills me up with a loving embrace.

When I look at you I see a friend,
someone I trust and love,
the time each day I spend with you,
just never seems enough.

I love each day we spend together,
these days just warm me so,
but what I love the most of all,
is the future that we hold.

This friendship that I feel,
can not be explained at times,
it just begins and ends each day with you,
our souls forever entwined.

So when I stare and look at you,
it's to fill my soul with love,
these feeling that come into my heart,
will never leave or depart.

Personal Emotions

_____

_____

_____

_____

_____

_____

_____

_____

_____

_____

_____

_____

_____

_____

_____

_____

_____

_____

_____

_____

_____

"GESTURES OF LOVE"

To give or show an act of love,
can mean the difference between two souls.
A gesture that makes your heart pound and glow
is something we all should know.

But how often do we mistake what we get,
as a slant designed to fool,
or how are our gestures of love that we give,
can be lost inside some crazy rule.

If love is what you want
then show the love you need,
with gestures of feelings that come from inside,
and express what you truly believe.

When you receive a gesture,
don't measure it by the quality that you gave,
just see where the feelings are coming from,
with a smile that says everything is okay.

Gestures of Love are the things that we do,
from the information that is given to us,
it takes opened eyes to find that thing inside,
that wins you a place in a heart.

Personal Emotions

"BEAUTY"

If I could be a mirror and you could see what I see,
you would witness a vision of beauty,
that your birth was meant to be.

I sometimes stare and see a dream,
as I look so close at you,
and blink real hard to let me know,
that this dream has come quite true.

You have a beauty that you fail to see,
but it's there just the same,
I wish you could see it through my eyes
to realize and be amazed.

I wish I was a mirror
that would reflect just what I love for me,
and let you witness the beauty of what,
my heart can truly see.

I am not a mirror,
but my love is there for you,
so always seek to see my eyes,
their reflection will surely tell you.
You have a beauty that is with you,
that only I can see,
so use me as your mirror each day
and share this love that I see.

Personal Emotions

"CARESS A HEART"

To caress a heart begins at the eyes,
as you look deep down inside.
You stare for awhile, as you gaze at the face,
that is beginning to offer a smile.

It takes some work to caress a heart,
that is waiting for your caring ways.
It starts with the parts that connect to the heart,
so be patient as you proceed on your way.

A listening ear, a hand held so tight,
or a hug at the right time of need,
gets you closer to be in
a position that ready to see.

To caress a heart before you take care of the parts,
will not make the person react,
so take all the time,
to figure and untwine,
and possibly start
with a massage on the back.

You'll know that it's felt,
the caress of the heart,
when the person gets close to your soul,
you both will feel the glow explode
from your head to your toes.

Personal Emotions

EXERCISES FOR GOOSEBUMPS

1. Talk openly about what you like about your partner's love toward
    you. It can include something that you remember many years
    ago that he or she is not doing presently.

    _____

    _____

    _____

    _____

    _____

2. Ask for something that would make you feel Goosebumps.

    _____

    _____

    _____

    _____

    _____

3. Think of something that you haven't done that you feel will
    bring Goosebumps to your partner.

    _____

    _____

    _____

    _____

    _____

Chapter Three
LOVING YOUR TIME
TOGETHER

Loving your time together might sound simple, however, for a lot of people or couples, it is not easy. The uneasiness that happens is not a signal that love is gone or that you have problems. What is being suggested is that you maybe are a "too complacent toward your partner", type of person.

Relationships need their space. Smothering someone constantly with loving demands can have the opposite effect on how your partner feels when they are around you. Loving your time together is how you nurture the moments you have to yourselves. Giving your mate his or her space without conditions is one of the most loving acts a person can do.

When you give, give unconditionally. Men, if your wife has household chores, or errands that need running, try to help or go with her and share that time. Women, the same applies to you. If your partner has things he needs to do that your company wouldn't interfere with, offer to go with him. While you're out, make it a date of sorts. Do your chores and have lunch, or go to a movie. There are no rules that say you can't work and play at the same time.

I love helping my wife shop for clothing. She trusts my tastes and realizes I am a lot more honest than a salesperson who thinks the ugliest pieces of clothing look good. I've learned over the years that women can't truly see their beauty, like men can.

Women carry around with them a "fun-house" mirror and see flaws that are not really there. It is important for a man to be involved and let the love of his life know how he sees her beauty. She might not totally agree, but she will get those Goosebumps we've been talking about.

So the examples given so far are making love. Sex, when the time is right, will be the greatest you'll ever experience, if you attempt to make love all year long. Your bodies will meld in such a way that will open your heart to what true love is all about.

I experience this everyday and I have never gotten bored with being a perpetual lover. Try to make a list of things you feel you can do with each other that in the past has been done separately. Think of your partner as your best friend. What would you want to do with your best friend that would bring pleasure to your time together?

THINGS TO DO TOGETHER

1. _____
2. _____
3. _____
4. _____
5. _____
6. _____
7. _____
8. _____
9. _____
10. _____

"TIME WELL SPENT"

There are choices to make of how we spend our time, it should always involve our pleasures. And if you can share it with someone, it will be a special time that you'll always treasure.

From the moment we connected, my time focused on you, and the pleasure I felt inside, and today is the same, as I feel no pain, as we spend our time entwined.

For me it's time well spent, as I am mixing my pleasures with the love that's in my life, but the time we spend being each others best friends, makes our relationship so alive.

If I had the power to add hours to, the 24 hours we have in a day, I would add as much as I can and take you in my hand, and see it as a worthwhile field day.

My wish can not be, it's obvious to you and me, so I will work toward making our time be a great event, and continue to show as we journey and go, that our "Time will be Well Spent"

Personal Emotions

_____

_____

_____

_____

_____

_____

_____

_____

_____

_____

_____

_____

_____

_____

_____

_____

_____

_____

_____

_____

_____

_____

"A TRUSTING FRIEND"

There was a void in my life, as I could not find a friend to trust, building walls all around for me to feel, My years drifted by missing pleasures for my eyes, feeling anger and disgust.

When we first met, it was only in passing, but a spark ignited my heart, and the contact we had, for years while I was sad, turned into a friendship that had yearning.

When our past began to end, and new beginnings were needed for me, you appeared at my door. It became a moment to choose, that a new life with you could not lose, and I could finally be happy forevermore.

Our years have gone so fast and my love for you still lasts, and the romance never seems to be at an end, but the one thing I still feel and enjoy with so much zeal, is that you remain my best and trusting friend.

Personal Emotions

"THE PROMISE"

For better or worse is a cliché, that is used to bind two lives,
but a promise that states what will always be, will keep you
in love for life.

My promise to you, is to always respect, the woman you want to be,
and encourage you to do what you want to go through,
and be there so I can see.

I promise to share and infuse, a special kind of love,
that keeps us sharing our time, always taking note,
that our relationship can't be broke, and our future will
always interlock.

My promise to love and to be always there, is easy for me to fulfill,
but a promise to plan our daily and future demands,
takes a commitment I promise to do.

I will see that we have all the pleasures that can be and look for new
ones to enjoy, but the promise that I give, is to always want to live,
with you never feeling a void.

Personal Emotions

"SHARING MY PRIVATE TIME"

I have at times my inner thoughts,
that only I can see,
and seem to have you by my side to share them all with me.

They are quite private, but not to where, I need to be alone,
just having you so close at hand,
makes makes my private thoughts belong.

There are some times I drift into,
a quite kind of mood,
but never needing to be alone, you need it understood.

I need you near throughout my day,
no matter what I reflect,
I want to share my private times if not, I'll feel neglect.

You are a part of my inner thoughts
and are there when I feel closed,
you are a pillow soft and warm, my privacy only knows.

So don't think that I need my space,
you never seem to invade,
and please keep sharing my private times each and everyday.

Personal Emotions

"CHALLENGE YOUR RELATIONSHIP"

If you wait for things to happen, it will never come,
but if you attempt to challenge it, the fun has just begun.
A relationship has rules to follow that are similar to rules you know,
you just have to see it that way, and watch it begin to grow.

When partners wait to receive the love,
or wait for results to appear,
the relationship becomes a challenge
and could possibly disappear.

So challenge yourself to be the one,
to invest your efforts well,
you'll find that this relationship will
be better than a "wishing well."

In life it takes an effort from you,
to get the things you want,
and once you apply it to your love,
the relationship will never give up.

I will always challenge myself, to keep our relationship strong,
and only ask that you participate, that's how I want you to belong.
So when you see me think of ways to bring fun and pleasure to our lives,
it's only me challenging our relationship to have it stay alive.

Personal Emotions

"TWO ROMANTIC SOULS"

*It's an embrace like no other,
two romantic souls share,
everyday as their love grows taller
they need to be alert and aware.*

*They search for the pleasures
that feed them deep inside,
for happiness is their food,
they are in a secret world
they only know,
they seem to always be amused.*

*Not much needs to be said
except expressions of love,
and the telling of how each continues to feel.
it's reaffirmed all day with the warmth in their hearts
to make their love remain so real.*

*Two Romantic Souls,
is a gift to the world,
as they only give rays of their love,
they welcome all in,
to their wonderful den,
with the invitation that fits like a glove.*

Personal Emotions

_____

_____

_____

_____

_____

_____

_____

_____

_____

_____

_____

_____

_____

_____

_____

_____

_____

_____

_____

_____

_____

_____

"MELDED AS ONE"

As our relationship grows along with our love,
I meld so close to you,
it seems as if we're in the same mind thought,
I can't stop thinking how much I love you.

I sense your thoughts; you hear my silent wishes,
we laugh at this spooky sense,
but what we both seem to always agree,
is that our melding is not nonsense.

It's almost an instant, the capture of your thoughts,
and how I know what you will say,
and before I utter my first words,
you respond in a magical way.

This is more than love or companionship,
this relationship we both seem to have,
it's like the merging of two souls,
into one that's always happy and glad.

There is a time we feel our pain
and react with love and care,
and embrace each other as if we were,
ONE that is removing all of the fear.

I can't imagine how much more we can meld,
but each day surprises me so,
it makes a new day exciting and fun,
being able to witness our glow.

Personal Emotions

"JUST LIKE BOOKENDS"

We seem to match up, like a paired set,
with similarities that only we can see,
we are like two bookends supporting our relationship,
as if it was meant to be.

Each Bookend does its part to keep our love in place
and not let things flop down on our shelf,
we are not interested in making any mistakes.

Each Bookend is unique, but came from a set,
that only will work upon our shelf,
and each bookend seems to know its job,
of how to support ourselves.

There are times when we're alone
and things just want to start to slide,
and we wonder if all will fall down and expose
a negative vulnerable side.

So when you see our bookends
upon our unique shelf of life
we have to understand that our love is strong
and will always turn out all right.

Personal Emotions

"MY LIFE WITH YOU"

Each day I thank God,
that you came into my life,
a rebirth was created that day,
the experiences that I have are inside my heart,
and they get better each and everyday.

I wouldn't have missed this for the world,
it's more than I deserve,
my life with you is so for real
I am gliding like a bird.

The glow that you have,
and warm rays I receive,
is a value that can't be described,
so please understand,
that I have become who I am,
from the care and the love of being by your side.

If this is the best that I will ever receive,
then I am a rich and lucky man,
because no one around has a friend such as you,
and I will say it over and over again.

Personal Emotions

Chapter Four
NEVER LET THE PASSION STOP

Being a Perpetual Lover will not cause you physical harm. Living the Mind Diet life with your partner, the person you love dearly, can only improve the standard of living you already have.

Think how lucky you are that you can love someone and be loved in return. Think about how growing old will be as you never stop your daily love making.

One of the most positive things a couple can do is plan their future, living each day that will build toward their goals. We do not know our future or when our time on Earth will end, but the unknown should not prevent you from making plans.

I'd rather live a hundred days making love all day long, than to waste my life afraid to open up not allowing the pleasures of my partner to enter my soul. Each day is one more step toward a future that is unknown.

If you've been hurt badly before, or had your heart broken after you've opened up completely, force yourself to get back up and try again. No one should live in a relationship that is not filled with passion, no matter what your past scars have done to you.

We were born with the ability to make choices, so why not choose to make love all year long? Why not become a perpetual lover? Afraid to take chances could be a sign that you are afraid you could not handle the pain of a breakup. Or you might be thinking it is easier to just get by and not take risks. But, isn't it true that your past pains were learning experiences that taught you to learn to live life to its fullest?

I believe that one has to give every relationship 110%, no matter how many bad relationships someone has had. I was in a twenty-one year marriage that had no passion for me, that was extremely dysfunctional. After I made the hardest decision, divorce, I did not hide away from getting involved again with a woman, even though the divorce almost wiped me out. Financially and emotionally I was determined to keep trying to find the dream relationship that I always wanted.

I know for a fact that my attitude helped me find my present wife, Nancy. I've been with her for twelve years, married almost nine and have never been happier in my life.

For a relationship to work each day you have to have the mindset of making love every moment. It has to become perpetual. I recommend becoming best friends with your partner. If you are not best friends now, work toward it. As we all get older our bodies change and what was one way of making love, will become another way of making love. But, it won't happen if you are not friends.

I want this book and this final chapter to be your new beginning forever with the person you love. Be creative, be spontaneous and don't forget to communicate. Before you read the final three poems, I'd like you to make a few more lists. This last exercise will hopefully, become a love contract that will be a lasting reminder of your love and commitment to Make Love All Year Long and become Perpetual Lovers.

WHAT I AM MOST AFRAID OF IN OUR RELATIONSHIP

1. _____

2. _____

3. _____

4. _____

5. _____

6. _____

7. _____

8. _____

9. _____

10. _____

WHAT I LOVE THE MOST ABOUT OUR RELATIONSHIP

1. _____
2. _____
3. _____
4. _____
5. _____
6. _____
7. _____
8. _____
9. _____
10. _____

WHAT ARE MY BIGGEST DREAMS FOR OUR RELATIONSHIP?

1. _____
2. _____
3. _____
4. _____
5. _____
6. _____
7. _____
8. _____
9. _____
10. _____

As I said in the beginning of this book, you and your partner will be making a promise to each other that will be signed and dated. Relationships do not always run smoothly and can hit many bumps along the way.

Making a loving promise to the relationship and each other helps keep the bond and the love strong. This is your final expression of how you feel toward the person you love, make it an emotionally strong promise that will never allow anything to come between the love you two have for each other.

I MAKE THIS PROMISE TO YOU

_____

_____

_____

_____

_____

_____

_____

_____

_____

_____

_____

_____

_____

_____

_____

_____

_____   _____
Signature   Date

I MAKE THIS PROMISE TO YOU

_____

_____

_____

_____

_____

_____

_____

_____

_____

_____

_____

_____

_____

_____

_____

_____

_____

_____   _____
Signature   Date

"THE LUCKIEST MAN ALIVE"

To dream and hope for a love like ours, can make for unhappy days, but I continue to live the dream, having you with me everyday.

When I see some people, who have given up on their quest for happiness and love, I understand that I have become the "Luckiest Man" who's life is filled with love.

I treasure our life, and who you are, and what you mean to me, and will do what I feel is my part, to return what I receive. Never doubt,or think I feel, less than what I've said, there is no other in my life, that I care to share my bed.

I have no need to search for wealth or riches of material things, I have the greatest asset in the world and I'm proud to wear our ring. Lets always remember that seeing the world takes not a lot of money, but eyes and heart with love inside, to experience the wonderful journey.

I am the luckiest man alive to have you in my life, and became the richest of them all when you became my wife. A wife is not the only thing I have with you today, you are my partner and best friend wrapped up as one each day.

As days go by and life's stresses appear and a pressure builds inside, I will think how lucky I've become, to have you by my side. I love you so it will always be and I thank you for your care, and I will always count how lucky I am each and every year.

Personal Emotions

"THE MAGIC OF 'THE KISS'"

It's a force that drives us all the time,
the need to do "The Kiss."
It's uncontrolled and needs release,
from feelings that can't be missed.

Sometimes it's just mixed with a hug,
or a friendly meeting hello,
but it's "The Kiss" that we do the best,
to express how our feelings show.

You start it slow, with gentle strokes,
your lips just soft and moist,
to where you both begin to touch,
your hands show a rejoice.
Sometimes your eyes remain real tight,
you're in your private dream state,
but sometimes you sneak a needed peek,
to make sure these feelings are not fake.

No matter how you greet a friend,
or someone you love so dear,
the way you do the magic of "The Kiss"
breaks down all emotions of fear.
It is your way to create a mood,
for the time you spend that day,
so be expressive with "The Kiss"
you're in control that way.

Personal Emotions

"MY TREASURED FRIEND"

From the beginning a relationship was formed,
a bond that stuck all these years,
building a foundation of love that's inside,
that I've cherished for so many years.

You are a friend that means more to me,
no words can express those thoughts,
you stoke our flame each day you're around
with the warmth of who you are.

I found a buried treasure, from a map I kept by my side,
it took me way too long to find you,
as I remained hidden with tears deep inside.

I call you friend, which means more to me
than a wife or lover can be,
I will always treasure the friendship we have, for all of eternity.

Personal Emotions

"A FRIEND, LOVER, AND WIFE"

It has been awhile since we became friends,
the beginnings seem distant at times.
We've had our pains along the way,
our hearts have been tested real hard.

No matter how hard the world seems at times,
when darkness just wants to consume,
I look in your eyes and see that special friend that I know
that continues to shine on through.

As Lover you've been more than I've needed,
but don't take away what you give.
I love how you've blossomed and grown as a woman,
your beauty keeps growing as it should.
The Lover you've become blends with the friend,
that I treasure so dear to my heart,
and I will be there every day and every year
to allow us to never be apart.

The wife that you are is the contract we have
that tells me my life is a true fact.
I'll always remain in your debt for the time
that you decided to call me back.

Your Friend, Lover and Husband

Personal Emotions

_____

_____

_____

_____

_____

_____

_____

_____

_____

_____

_____

_____

_____

_____

_____

_____

_____

_____

_____

_____

_____

"AN ANNIVERSARY BLESSING"

How can it be this love I feel,
it's stronger than when we met,
It keeps on growing inside my heart,
each day feels like an event.

I see our past it's love so strong,
it makes today a treasured gift,
but most of all I see our future
filled with joy that just won't quit.

The gifts I bring each day to you,
come from the feelings that are deep within my soul,
and I wrap them with the ribbons of my love
through the words and feelings I need to show.

You are a blessing that I thank you for,
to be in my world so bright,
you make each day I have with you
be the event I call my life.

Personal Emotions

WHAT TO DO NEXT?

Like most projects we finish, the work gets put upon a shelf. This loving and caring effort is not one of those endeavors that have been completed.

As a couple, you have been shown a method to enhance your relationship and the Mind Diet Program must be accomplished continuously. Once you have a beautiful garden with a rainbow of colors, you do not stop watering or fertilizing it. That is what you have to do to keep your love from dying and becoming stale.

Keep this book out where both of you can see it everyday. When you invent a new Goosebump put it inside your book. Remember this is a photo album of your relationship's love.

May you always Make Love Every Day and become a Perpetual Lover.

Personal Emotions

Personal Emotions

Personal Emotions

_____

_____

_____

_____

_____

_____

_____

_____

_____

_____

_____

_____

_____

_____

_____

_____

_____

_____

_____

_____

Personal Emotions

Beyond Valentine's Day - Making Love all Year Long

www.ingramcontent.com/pod-product-compliance
Lightning Source LLC
LaVergne TN
LVHW091157080426
835509LV00006B/736